Catherine

In collaboration with the Commi[illegible] [illegible] [illegible] [illegible]rical Study
of the Battle of Waterloo a.s.b.l. and the Wellington Museum, Waterloo

The little guide to the Battle of Waterloo

The little village of Waterloo

was linked to Brussels by a single paved road. Waterloo, around 20 km south of Brussels, and its surrounding region, was mainly agricultural. It was a rolling landscape, with many scattered villages, farms, fields, woods and windmills. Everything seemed calm there until the morning of June 18, 1815. Braine-l'Alleud, Genappe, Lasne and Waterloo would soon become no more than a battlefield.

Find the main farms: Hougoumont, Haie Sainte, Papelotte, ... which would become strategic points during the battle.

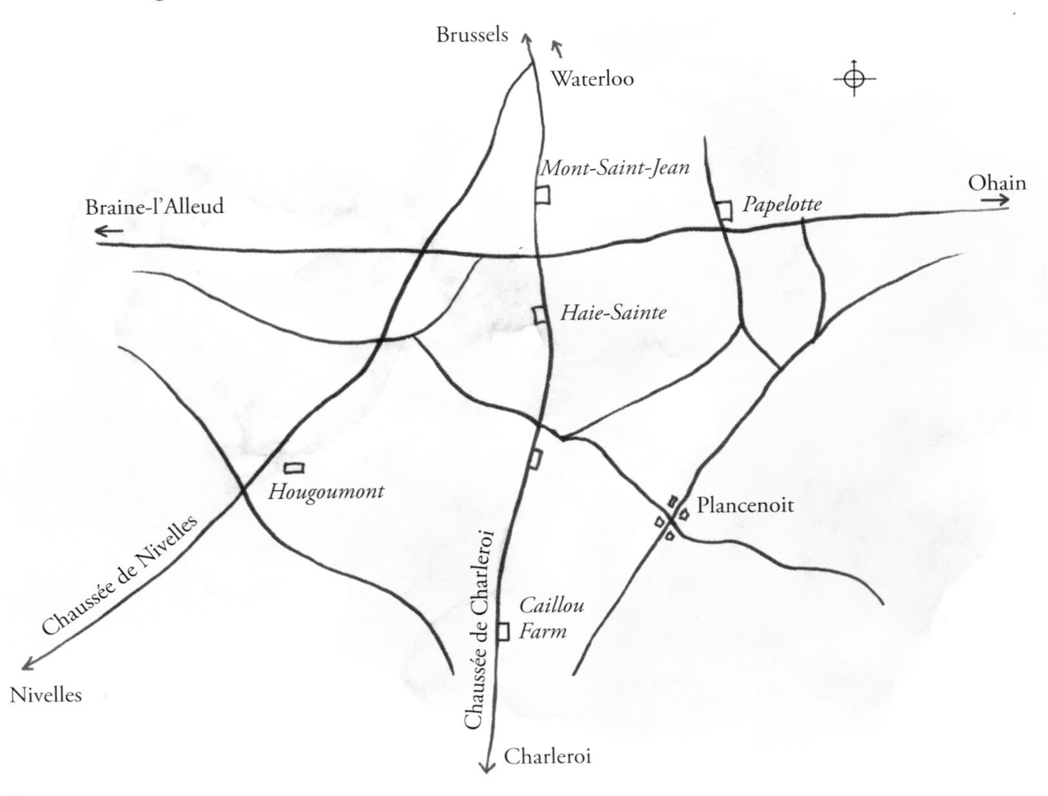

1815

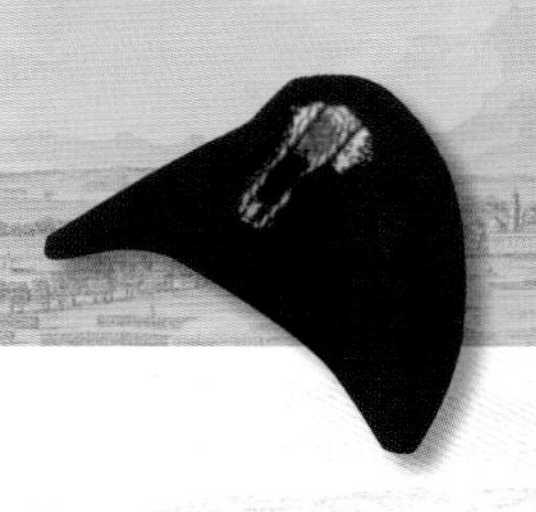

Europe under Napoleon

Napoleon built up his empire at the cost of many wars. Almost all the other European countries formed a coalition to try and defeat him. From 1813, the French empire began to collapse. In 1814, Napoleon was exiled to the island of Elba in Northern Italy. King Louis XVIII, in exile since 1792, became King of France, with the support of foreign armies.

The Hundred Days

The French, and in particular the French army, were not happy with Louis XVIII's new regime. Napoleon, who knew the King was unpopular, found an opportunity to seize power again. He escaped from Elba with a small troop of men, and landed in Golfe-Juan in the South of France on March 1, 1815. The troops sent to intercept and arrest him rebelled against the King. Napoleon was borne in triumph to Paris on March 20, 1815. Louis XVIII fled to Ghent in what is now Belgium. For 100 days, Napoleon was back in power. What was he going to do?

Napoleonic wars

Napoleon's abdication in 1814

Napoleon arrives in Golfe-Juan

THE BELGIAN CAMPAIGN

The European countries did not agree to Emperor Napoleon's return to power in France. They formed a new armed coalition ready to intervene. Nearly a million men gathered on the French borders.

On June 12, 1815, around 130,000 French soldiers left for war, to fight the alliance against Napoleon. Where were they heading? Belgium! Napoleon wanted to capture Brussels where two allied armies – the English and Prussian forces – were stationed on Belgian territory.

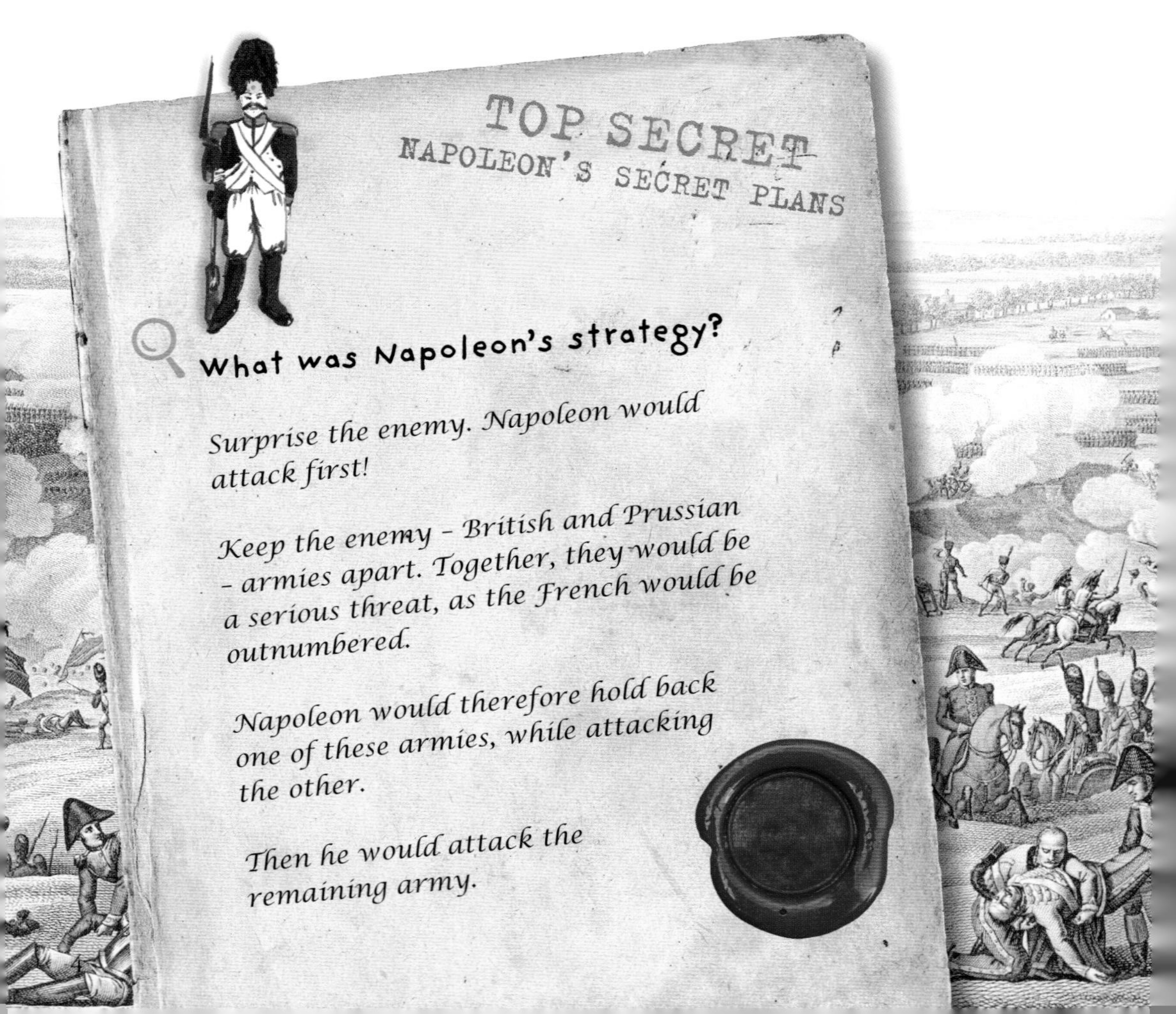

TOP SECRET
NAPOLEON'S SECRET PLANS

What was Napoleon's strategy?

Surprise the enemy. Napoleon would attack first!

Keep the enemy – British and Prussian – armies apart. Together, they would be a serious threat, as the French would be outnumbered.

Napoleon would therefore hold back one of these armies, while attacking the other.

Then he would attack the remaining army.

Who were the Allies?

The army commanded by Wellington was made up of British, Hanoverian and Dutch-Belgian troops. This army had around 94,000 men, while the Prussian army, under Marshal Blücher, had around 123,000 men.

See how Napoleon advanced towards Brussels. Where would he face the Allied armies?

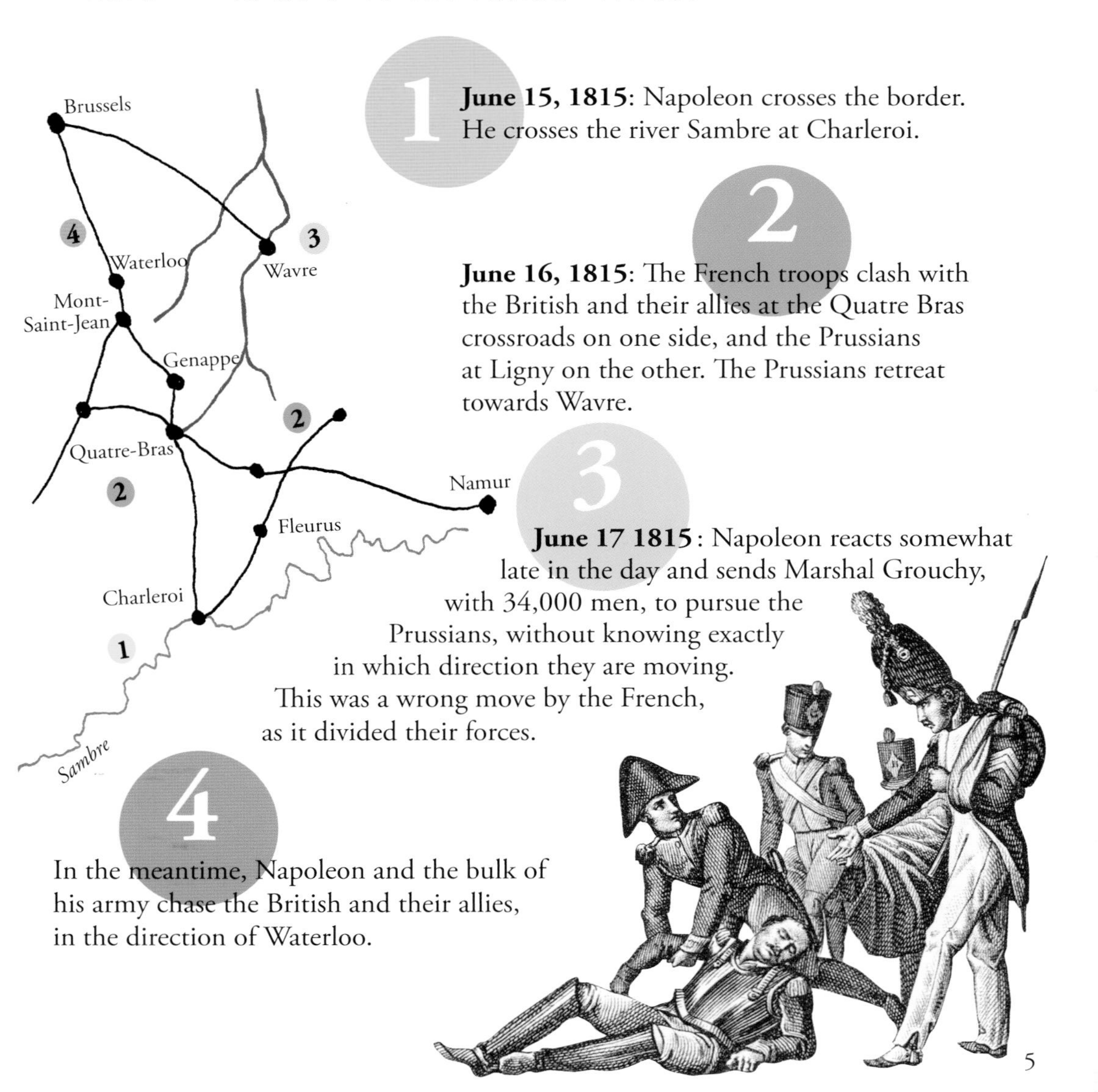

1

June 15, 1815: Napoleon crosses the border. He crosses the river Sambre at Charleroi.

2

June 16, 1815: The French troops clash with the British and their allies at the Quatre Bras crossroads on one side, and the Prussians at Ligny on the other. The Prussians retreat towards Wavre.

3

June 17 1815: Napoleon reacts somewhat late in the day and sends Marshal Grouchy, with 34,000 men, to pursue the Prussians, without knowing exactly in which direction they are moving. This was a wrong move by the French, as it divided their forces.

4

In the meantime, Napoleon and the bulk of his army chase the British and their allies, in the direction of Waterloo.

NAPOLEON

Napoleon Bonaparte was born in Ajaccio, Corsica in 1769. As a young soldier, he won many victories. Following a successful military takeover in 1799, he became France's First Consul. In 1804, he was declared Emperor of France. He was hugely ambitious and waged war against most European countries. However the major European powers resisted and wished to put a stop to the expansion of his powers. Having been defeated several times, Napoleon was exiled twice, the first time to the island of Elba, and then again to Saint Helena in the middle of the Atlantic Ocean, where he died in 1821 at the age of 52.

This is the Emperor Napoleon. Find his bicorne (cocked hat).

RECORD
Napoleon won 69 battles out of 75!

Imperial Eagle
Napoleon chose the eagle to symbolise his imperial power. The figure of an eagle was carried above the French flag.

CAILLOU FARM

June 17, 1815, Caillou Farm

Napoleon set up his headquarters in a farm, from which the owners had fled the previous day. Caillou Farm is in Vieux-Genappe, a few kilometres to the south of Waterloo. On the day after the battle, the Prussians set fire to the farm, Napoleon's last headquarters. The barn had been transformed into a military hospital and housed the many wounded, who would perish in the fire.

It had been raining hard and the terrain was very muddy. On the morning of the battle, Napoleon took a look around the area, accompanied by a local guide. Can you see them? The Emperor called a meeting of his officers to give his orders. His objective was to take the Mont-Saint-Jean crossroads.

Where is Napoleon on the morning of the Battle of Waterloo? Find him in this picture. What is he doing?

WELLINGTON

Arthur Wellesley, Duke of Wellington, was born in Ireland in 1769. He was Anglo-Irish. A British politician and soldier, he was Commander-in-Chief of the troops occupying France in 1814. He was a good defending soldier and led various campaigns, particularly in Portugal and Spain, where he managed to hold back a number of Napoleon's armies. In 1830, Wellington was involved in the creation and independence of a buffer State, Belgium. He died in 1852.

What uniform is the Duke of Wellington wearing?

SCOOP
Wellington and Napoleon were both 45 the year of the Battle of Waterloo.

COACHING INN HEADQUARTERS

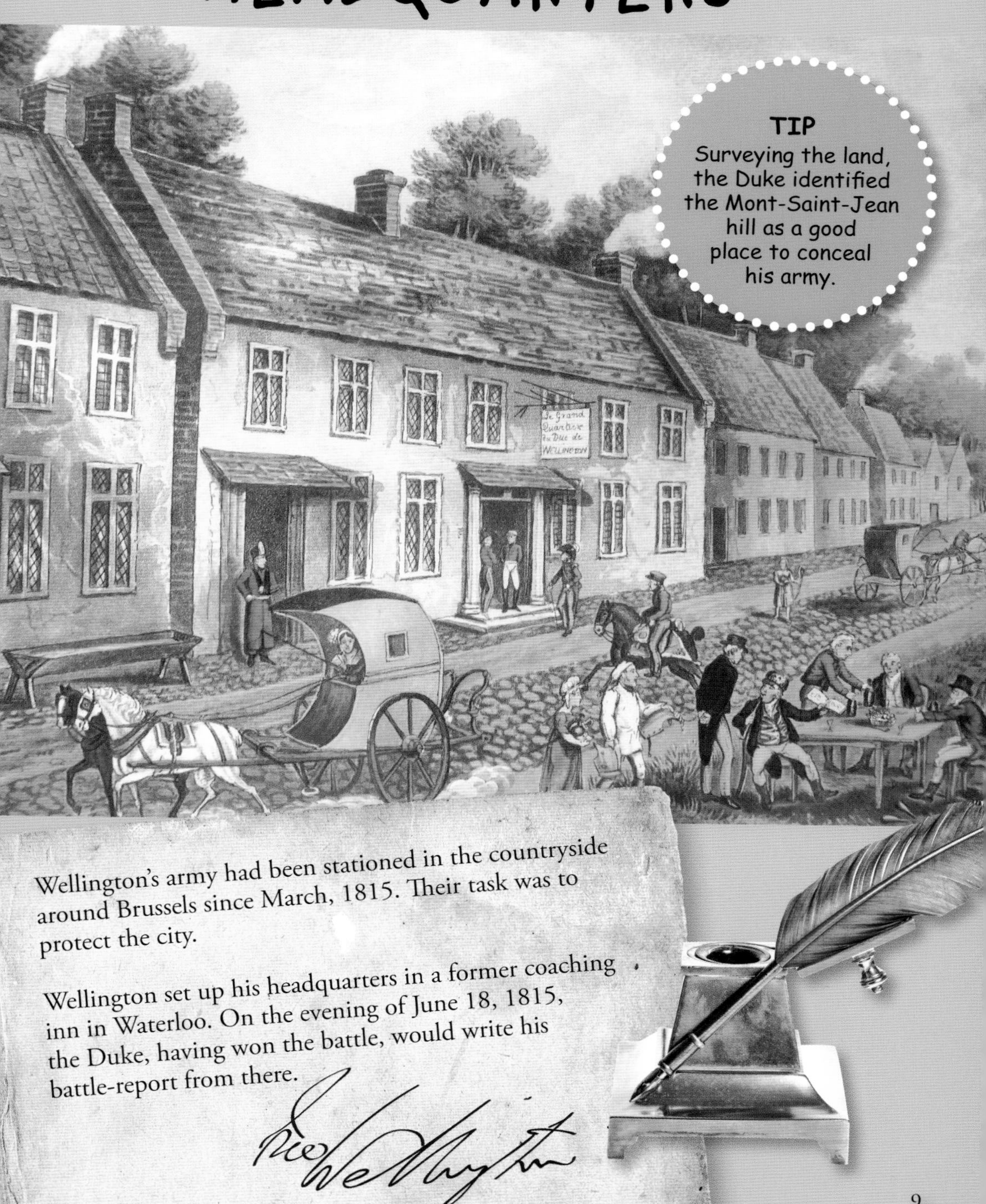

TIP
Surveying the land, the Duke identified the Mont-Saint-Jean hill as a good place to conceal his army.

Wellington's army had been stationed in the countryside around Brussels since March, 1815. Their task was to protect the city.

Wellington set up his headquarters in a former coaching inn in Waterloo. On the evening of June 18, 1815, the Duke, having won the battle, would write his battle-report from there.

BLÜCHER

Gebhard Leberecht von Blücher, Prince of Wahlstatt, was born in 1742 in Rostock, on the shores of the Baltic opposite Denmark. He was a General and Field Marshal – the highest rank in the Prussian army – and had fought in the French Revolutionary wars, and the wars against Napoleon at the time of the First Empire.

A sabre is a type of sword with a long, pointed blade, curved on the sharp side.

What is Blücher holding under his arm?

SCOOP
Marshal Blücher was an old man of 73 at the time of the Battle of Waterloo. His role was crucial. His nickname was 'Marshall Vorwärts': 'Marshal Forwards'!

Prussia was the former State of Northern Germany.

PRESBYTERY

June 15, 1815, Sombreffe presbytery

After the fighting on June 15, 1815 in Charleroi, General Blücher moved his headquarters (HQ) from Namur to Sombreffe, in the local presbytery (the vicarage). He spent the night of the 15th of June, 1815 there. Blücher was angry because his troops did not arrive soon enough to position themselves in good time, so struck the door several times with his sabre. The marks can still be seen today.

TIP
Throughout the battle, this presbytery was the HQ of the Prussian army. As it was near the church, the officers could find it easily by following the way to the church-tower.

Draw your own headquarters, making sure it's close to a landmark which can be seen from several kilometres away.

DUCHESS'S BALL

June 15, 1815, the Duchess of Richmond's Ball

This glittering event brought together local Brussels and foreign high society. The Duke of Wellington and his officers attended the ball. Waltzes and quadrilles were danced. The young people chattered away happily. It is said that a Prussian officer burst into the ball and announced discreetly that Napoleon's army had made a surprise crossing of the border and was advancing towards Charleroi in three columns. Calmly, the Duke of Wellington ordered his officers to leave the ball. In the streets, on the corners, drums and bagpipes sounded, calling officers back to the army to prepare for battle. Can you hear them?

Look at the women's dresses and the men's outfits. Are they wearing or carrying anything particular?

UNIFORM

The officers are wearing boots, stockings, hats and carrying sabres.

Look at the uniforms.
What would you choose to wear to the ball?
Draw your Empire-style outfit.

QUATRE-BRAS

Victory for the Allies

Place: Quatre-Bras (Baisy-Thy) crossroads: where the Nivelles-Namur road intersects with the Charleroi-Brussels road
Day: June 16, 1815
Time: 14.00

The Battle of Quatre Bras

On the morning of June 16, 1815, the **Prince of Orange**, aged 22, is already there and waiting. Quatre Bras crossroads – a strategic hub – is around 40 km south of Brussels.

The Prince of Orange

Around 9.30: **Wellington** arrives on horseback at Quatre Bras. From there, the British army and its allies can stay in communication with Marshal Blücher, stationed near Ligny, and can cut the French off from the road to Brussels.

At 14.00: There is intense fighting between the French, under **Marshal Ney**, and the British and their allies. The French at first seem to have the upper hand, but reinforcements arrive – **Picton**'s division and the Brunswick Corps from Genappe. Helped by the Dutch-Belgian cavalry, Wellington recovers control of the situation.

Around 15.00: Napoleon sends a despatch to **Ney**, ordering him to take the crossroads, in order to join the French army fighting the Prussians at Ligny, and to prevent them moving off northwards. But Ney, who has received no reinforcements, is not able to capture the crossroads, despite several French cavalry attacks on the British squares. By the evening of the battle, the British control the crossroads.

Marshal Ney

He was known as the 'Bravest of the Brave', because of his courage, shown during the many battles in which he fought at the time of the French Revolution and the Empire. After Waterloo he was accused of treason by the restored royalist government, and put to death in Paris on December 8, 1815.

LIGNY

Victory for the French

The Battle of Ligny

Napoleon arrives from Fleurus with most of his army (68,000 men) to confront the Prussians, who have taken up position in Ligny and Saint-Amand. **Wellington**, busy at Quatre Bras, cannot help the Prussians, who are faced with the bulk of the French army. After fierce fighting, the French gradually get the upper hand. Ligny is finally taken by the French. Evening falls, Blücher attacks once again, but the Prussians have to retreat.

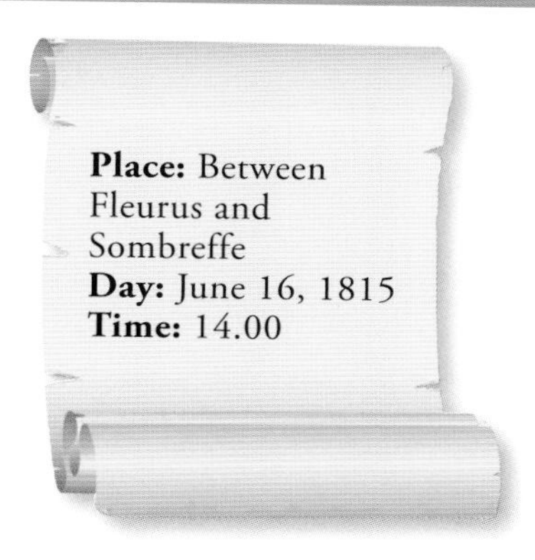

Place: Between Fleurus and Sombreffe
Day: June 16, 1815
Time: 14.00

General von Gneisenau, Blücher's Chief of Staff, organises a falling back towards Wavre, to the north, to stay on the same line as Wellington. The Prussians have kept their artillery almost completely intact, and have maintained a fighting spirit. The Prussian army is beaten but not defeated! Napoleon, however, thinks that the Prussians are out of action. The French, exhausted, don't pursue them further.

Where is Blücher? Can you see him?

SCOOP

At the last Prussian charge, Blücher's horse is killed. The old Marshal falls and narrowly escapes capture.

June 18… The Battle of Waterloo is just beginning!

Three armies (around 200,000 men) will fight each other for nearly 10 hours in an area of about 5 x 4 km.

The British and allied armies occupy the area between the Farm-Castle of Hougoumont and Papelotte Farm (see map p. 2), and also have men at the centre of the line at Haie Sainte Farm. These troops are also protected by a ridge, which partially hides them from the French. **Blücher**, at Wavre, informs Wellington that he will join him during the course of the day. His army moves towards Ohain, Chapelle-Saint-Lambert. He leaves one corps in Wavre to stop **Grouchy** from advancing. But Napoleon thinks that the Prussians will not take part in the battle at Waterloo. A fatal error!

First French attack

The Farm-Castle of Hougoumont acted as protection for the right flank of Wellington's army. At 11.30, **Prince Jérôme Bonaparte**, Napoleon's younger brother, launches the first attack against the British at Hougoumont Farm.

Place: Around Hougoumont Farm
Day: June 18, 1815
Time: 11.30

HOUGOUMONT

British victory

The attack on Hougoumont is only supposed to be a diversionary attack, but Jérôme insists on trying to capture the farm-castle, and causes the unnecessary deaths of many French soldiers during the fighting, which lasts all day. Although the barns, stables and some of the buildings are set on fire, the farm-castle stays in the hands of the British and their allies.

The Little Drummer boy
It is said that of the Frenchmen who manage to enter the farm, the only one spared is the young French drummer boy.

A French giant! Lieutenant Legros smashes through one of the gates with a series of axe-blows. However the French are pushed back in hand-to-hand fighting and the gate closes back on them.

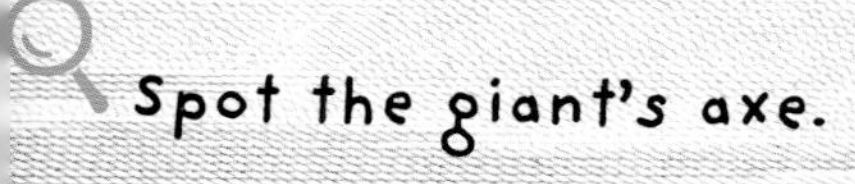

SCOOP
The title of 'the bravest man of the battle' went to Corporal James Graham, who closed the gates of Hougoumont farm, and thus contributed to the victory. He shared this honour with Colonel Macdonald.

The gate is closed against the French attackers.

PAPELOTTE

French victory

Place: South east of Waterloo
Day: June 18, 1815
Time: 13.30

Papelotte Farm

Papelotte Farm, to the east of the Duke of Wellington's line of defence, was occupied by the British and their allies. With Hougoumont and Haie Sainte, it was the third farm to be used by Wellington's army, as it served both the Prussian and the Anglo-Dutch troops. It was occupied briefly by the French troops. Partially burnt down during the battle, it has been rebuilt, with an octagonal tower.

Rebuild the farm, which has been badly damaged during the fighting. How do you think it should look?

ARTILLERY

In the cornfield, Napoleon's troops are setting up their grand battery. Heave-ho! The terrain is muddy and the artillerymen are pulling a huge cannon, a 12-piece.

Can you see General Dessales and his chief officers? What do you think they are doing?

13.30 : The French artillery, based opposite Belle Alliance Farm (see map p.2), open fire against the farm with their '**grand battery**' – made up of numerous cannons – for almost 40 minutes. Their objective: to weaken the Allies' centre-left flank before launching a major infantry attack.

14.00: To the east, you can just make out the Prussian army approaching Ohain.

14.30 : The **French infantry** attack begins. Around 20,000 men rush to the top of the hill occupied by the British and their allies. When they are nearly there, the French are brutally stopped in their tracks by the English infantrymen. The **English cavalry** charge forward. The French infantry are not able to form a square to resist them. Chaos sets in. Two or three thousand men are taken prisoner, two flags (the eagles) are captured and two horse-batteries are put out of action.

HAIE SAINTE

Victory for the Allies, then the French

Place: Close to the village of Plancenoit
Day: June 18, 1815
Time: 14.30

Haie Sainte Farm

A key position for the Allies, at the centre of their line of defence.

14.30: Under **Marshal Ney**, the French try to capture Haie Sainte Farm, which is occupied by Hanoverians, from a detachment of the *King's German Legion*. Fierce fighting takes place here throughout the day.

17.30: Napoleon orders Ney to attack once again. The barn catches fire. The French climb onto the roof of the pigsty and enter the courtyard. The Hanoverians, short of ammunition, have to leave the farm. Soon the French, victorious, also take the sand quarry opposite the farm. This allows the French artillery to bombard Wellington's centre, which loses many of its men.

SCOTLAND FOREVER!

The cavalry attack

The French infantry, attempting to break through the centre of the allied lines, is harassed by the British, sowing disorder in its ranks. Amidst fearful noise and the thick smoke of the firearms, the British squadrons then attack the French 'grand battery', made up of many cannons. They ignore calls to rally. What are they thinking of?

**Can you hear the stampeding and the cries?
The Scottish horsemen cry out as they charge forward, to give themselves courage and, above all, to intimidate the enemy.**

CAVALRY

French victory

15.30: Counter-attack by the French cavalry
Napoleon, attentive to the course of the battle, orders his best lancers to launch a side-attack against the British cavalry, which narrowly escapes being wiped out and is scattered.

16.00: Ney decides, without orders from Napoleon, to launch an attack by part of the French cavalry against the Allies. The British infantry, on Wellington's orders, draw back behind the crest of the hill and form a square. The French cavalry attack surprises Napoleon himself: 'It's an hour too early!', but he sends 5,000 extra horsemen to support the charge. These are met by volleys of grapeshot, and then by on-going fire from the British infantry. Their sabres cannot help them!

SCOOP
For two hours, Ney tries to push back the enemy, with at least 9 cavalry charges, but in vain.

SQUARE

A square (with 4 sides, each around 20 metres long) is one way of positioning an infantry battalion of 600 men. They move into the square formation in response to an enemy cavalry charge. The men line up in 3 or 4 rows, with their bayonets facing outwards. In this way they form a wall of steel blades to frighten the horses, which rear up. The square protects the officers, the wounded, the flags and the gunners. This is how the English were able to withstand charges by the French cavalry. Some squares were charged at nine to twelve times.

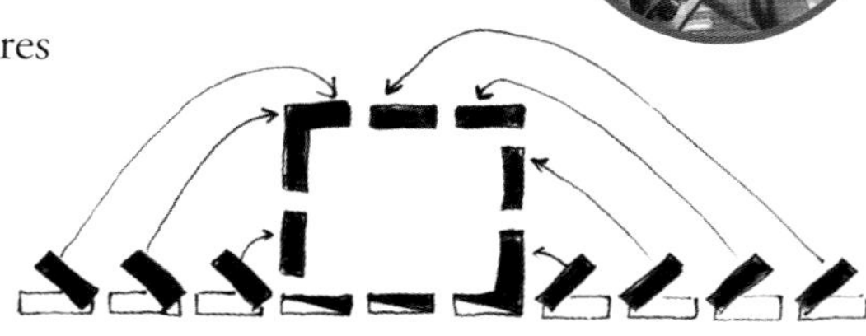

See how a square is formed from a line of infantrymen.

How are the horses reacting to the square?

PLANCENOIT

French victory

Place: Village of Plancenoit, near Lasne
Day: June 18, 1815
Time: 16.30

Village of Plancenoit

The Prussians arrive, emerging from the Paris woods. They march towards Belle Alliance Farm (see map p.2) to take the French from behind. The French resist, but cannot stop the Prussians entering the village. There are 20,000 Prussians, 6,000 French infantrymen and 2,000 French cavalrymen.

The village is on fire! Look at the Prussians attacking Plancenoit.

TEARING EACH OTHER APART!

Prussian victory

18.00 : The Prussians bombard the village of Plancenoit. The French army, at risk of being surrounded, resists, since losing Plancenoit would mean losing the battle. Throughout the fighting, the Prussians receive reinforcements, while Napoleon brings in his Old Guard - an elite unit - to support his Young Guard, which is completely outnumbered. After tough fighting, the French rout the Prussians. A temporary French victory.

19.30 : There are now 36,000 Prussians, against 15,000 Frenchmen.

How are the marksmen protecting themselves?

COUNTER-ATTACK ON THE HAIE SAINTE

18.30: After many attempts, the French manage to take control of Haie Sainte Farm, but the outcome of the battle is still uncertain....

19.00: Now the Prussians have reached the battlefield, and the Allied armies far outnumber the French army! Blücher's troops threaten the right wing and the supply line of Napoleon's army.
To counter this threat, Napoleon orders his Imperial Guard to attack.

Fatal order!
Behind the farm, **Colon Ompteda** receives orde from the Prince of Orar to retake Haie Sainte Fa Ompteda, realising the f of this instruction, tries change the Prince's min but without success. He leads his men in the attack. Ompteda i killed, with most of his men.

THE IMPERIAL GUARD

Napoleon brings in his last fresh troops. Nine battalions of the Imperial Guard, to fight Wellington's troops, reinforced by the Dutch-Belgian troops. Napoleon spreads a rumour that **Grouchy** is arriving with reinforcements. The first attack is led by **Marshal Ney**; the second group waits in reserve at the foot of the Belle Alliance plateau. The Imperial Guard is weakened by hails of grapeshot. Wellington has huge fire-power.

Place: Plateau around the Belle Alliance, at Lasne
Day: June 18, 1815
Time: 19.30

Look at the uniform of these grenadiers, a soldier and officers in the Napoleon's elite Imperial Guard.

The Imperial Guard
were the Emperor's special reserve troops. The Guard was made up of elite soldiers on whom Napoleon could rely on in all circumstances. Its task was to protect the Emperor. At Waterloo, however, the guard was called in as a reinforcement and had to fight.

UXBRIDGE

Find Wellington and Uxbridge. Who is that lying on a stretcher in Hussar uniform?

During the French attacks, General **Uxbridge** – commander of the British cavalry – was beside Wellington when he was hit by a cannonball which broke his leg. His leg had to be amputated, and from then on he wore an articulated artificial limb, which can still be seen at the Wellington Museum.

FINAL SQUARE

Every man for himself!

21.00: The French are routed. The French retreat and flee in the direction of Genappe. One last square of French grenadiers resists and holds up the pursuing allied troops.

Marshal Grouchy never reaches the battlefield. Despite the sound of cannons, and without any precise orders, he carries on pursuing the Prussian rear-guard to Wavre (see map p.5). After the Emperor's defeat, he brings all his wounded back to France. On the way back, he fights on at Namur.

BELLE ALLIANCE FARM

Place: Farm in Lasne
Day: June 18, 1815
Time: 21.30

Wellington and Blücher meet

By the evening of June 18, the Allies have won the Battle of Waterloo. The Duke of Wellington and Field-Marshal Blücher meet at the Belle-Alliance and congratulate each other on the outcome of the battle.

The two victorious leaders shake hands and speak for around ten minutes. The key to their success was that they were in contact throughout the battle and were able to come to each other's aid. Blücher said only one word in French.

Imagine what the two victors are saying.

AFTER THE BATTLE

The Battle of Waterloo is referred to by various names! Do you know them?

And you, what name would you give the battle?

....

....

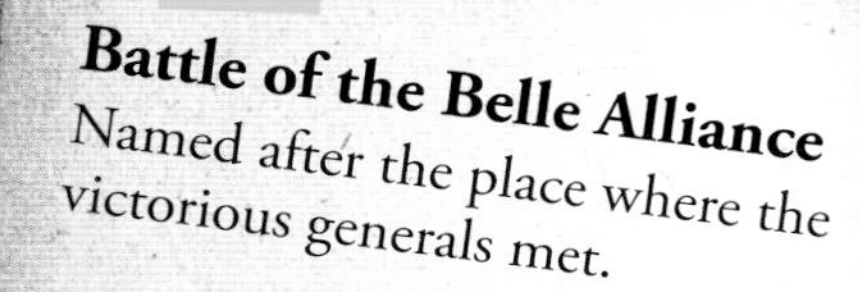

Battle of the Belle Alliance
Named after the place where the victorious generals met.

Battle of Mont-Saint-Jean
Since the British and Allied troops took refuge behind the Mont-Saint-Jean.

Battle of Waterloo
On the evening of the battle, Wellington wrote a report in his headquarters, and noted down where he was staying: Waterloo.

RECORD
Almost 200,000 soldiers took part, and around 10,000 were killed, including 5,000 Frenchmen. 30,000 were wounded, of which 20,000 were French.

The Treaty of Paris (20/11/1815)

The representatives of the victorious countries acted on the decisions concerning the new Europe taken at the **Congress of Vienna**. The Treaty of Paris, of **November 20, 1815**, drew up new borders for France, which had to pay large amounts in compensation to the victorious Allies. The treaty was designed to ensure that France would not again challenge the new outlines of Europe, and would not rebel against its restored monarchy.

The Holy Alliance

On **September 26, 1815**, the leaders of the winning countries formed the '*Holy Alliance*', to keep peace, but also to protect themselves against the liberal ideas inherited from the French Revolution.

Text and illustrations: Catherine de Duve
Concept and production: Kate'Art Editions
Layout: Véronique Lux
Technical review: Lucien Cécille and Committee for the Historical Study of the Battle of Waterloo a.s.b.l.
Translated by: Rachel Cowler

Wellington Museum, Waterloo:
P. 2: *The Bodenghien inn at Waterloo in 1816.* Aquatint etching by Charles Turner after Georges Jones – p. 7: *Caillou Farm.* Etching – p. 9: *Headquarters of the Duke of Wellington in the village of Waterloo,* 1817 – p. 25: *View of the village of Plancenois.* Lithograph by J. Sturm, after E. Pingret, published by Jobard – p. 29: *The meeting of Wellington and Blücher,* after the painting by J. Maclise – p. 30: *The Meeting of the Duke of Wellington and Field Marshal Blücher on the Evening of the Victory of Waterloo at La Belle Alliance.*

Other:
Cover, p. 6: *The Emperor Napoleon Bonaparte in his Study at the Tuileries,* 1812, *J.L.* David. National Gallery of Art, Washington – Cover: *Erection of the Lion's mound in Waterloo.* Lithograph by Jobard, after Bertrand – Cover: *The Lion of Waterloo* – Cover, p. 3: *Napoleon's Bicorne hat,* Royal Museum of the Armed Forces, Brussels – Cover, p. 21: *Scotland Forever,* 1881, E. Thompson. Leeds Museums and Galleries, Leeds – Cover, p. 26: *Ompteda in front of the farm La Haie Sainte* ©Patrice Courcelle – p. 1: *Battle of Wagram. 6th July 1806,* 1836, H. Vernet. National museum of the Palace of Versailles, Versailles – p. 2, p. 3, p. 4, p. 5, p. 10: *The Battle of Waterloo 1815,* C. Vernet. 19th century print. Private collection – p. 2, p. 15: *The Battle of Ligny,* 1875, E. Crofts – p. 2, p. 4, p. 7, p. 11, p. 17, p. 18, p. 24, p. 30: Illustrations ©Catherine de Duve – p. 3: *Napoleon leaving the island of Elba. 26 February 1815,* J. Baume. National museum of the Palace of Versailles, Versailles – p. 4: *Map of Belgium* – p. 4: *Napoleon's return from Elba,* 1818, C.A.G. Steuben – p. 5, p. 8: *Arthur Wellesley, 1st Duke of Wellington,* 1804, R. Home. National Portrait Gallery, London – p. 5, p. 10: *Marshal Blücher,* ca 1815-1819. Stiftung Stadtmuseum, Berlin – p. 6: *Imperial eagle.* Private collection-p.7: *The Morning of The Battle of Waterloo: The French await Napoleon's Orders,* 1876, E. Crofts. Sheffield Galleries and Museum Trust, Sheffield – p. 12, p. 13: *The Duchess of Richmond's Ball on the 15th June 1815,* R.A. Hillingford, 19th century, The Trustees of the Goodwood Collection – p. 14: *Marshal Ney,* F. Gérard. Army Museum, Paris – p. 14: *Portrait of the Prince of Orange,* 1854, C.P. Verhulst, Royal Museums of Fine Arts of Belgium, Brussels – p. 15: *The Fall of Blücher,* 1890, E. Hünten – p. 16: *Defence of the Château de Hougoumont,* D. Dighton. National Army Museum, London – p. 17: *Drum,* Royal Museum of the Armed Forces, Brussels – p. 17: *Closing the Gate at Hougoumont,* R. Gibb. National Museums of Scotland, Edinburgh – p. 17: *The attack on the North gate,* s.d., K. Rocco – p. 19: *Setting up the grand battery* ©Patrice Courcelle – p. 20: *The Defence of the Farm La Haye Sainte, A. Northern.* Niedersächsisches Landesmuseum, Hannover – p. 22: *Cavalry attack. Marshal Ney,* 1912, Detail from the Waterloo Panorama, Waterloo – p. 23: *Quatre Bras,* 1875, E. Thompson, E. Brassine collection. National Gallery of Victoria, Melbourne – p. 24: *The storming of Plancenoit,* 1843, L. Elsholtz – p. 25: *Attacking the Prussians in Plancenoit in the Battle of Waterlo*o, 1873, A. Northern. Hamburger Kunsthalle, Hamburg – p. 25: *The Prussian attack on Plancenoit.* Private collection – p. 27: *Grenadiers on foot. Officer and soldier (Imperial Guard),* 1843, H. Bellangé – p. 27: *Grenadier on horseback (Imperial Guard),* 1843, H. Bellangé – p. 28: *The Battle of Waterloo (Wellington and Uxbridge),* 1824, J.W. Pieneman, Rijksmuseum – p. 29: *The last square at Waterloo.* Private collection – p. 31: illustration, Lucie Hanquet.

With thanks to: Bernard Snoy, President, Lucien Cécille, Secretary and the members from Committee for the Historical Study of the Battle of Waterloo a.s.b.l., Etienne Claude, Director, Denis Piret and Véronique Maton from Wellington Museum, Daniel de Duve, Patrice Courcelle, Lucie Hanquet, Camille Ransquin, Benoit Sibille, Sandra Mangoubi, Véronique Lux, Martina Cappuccio, Ophélie Legast, Floriane, Gabriela and all the people who contributed to the making of this book.